Life in Ancient
GREECE

by Professor Michael Scott

Map of the Ancient Greek World

Ancient Greek city states, tribal areas and settlements

Persian Empire

ATLANTIC OCEAN

BRITAIN
FRANCE
SPAIN
ITALY
SICILY
Europe
Asia
Africa

Caspian Sea
Black Sea
Red Sea
Persian Gulf
Arabian Gulf
Mediterranean Sea

GREECE
LIBYA
EGYPT
AFGHANISTAN
PAKISTAN
INDIA
Indus

Ancient Greece

Aegean Sea
Adriatic Sea
MACEDON
Delphi
Olympia
Sparta
Athens
Bay of Marathon

N E S W

Contents

Uncovering Ancient Greece

How can we discover what happened over 2500 years ago in ancient Greece? There are lots of ways!

Clues to the Past

The ancient Greeks wrote histories, plays, poems and law court speeches. Many of these **texts** survived because they were copied out again and again by people who lived throughout the next 2000 years. **Archaeologists** in modern Greece dig up human and animal bones, gold and silver ornaments, toys, pots and pans, jewellery and coins. Buildings and pieces of art created by the ancient Greeks have survived, too.

An Ancient Sanctuary

Delphi was an important religious **sanctuary** for the ancient Greeks. Historians knew the importance of this place because lots of surviving texts talked about it. But the remains of Delphi's beautiful temples and buildings were completely buried underground.

A sanctuary was a place, building or group of buildings where people worshipped one or more gods. ▼

Ruins of the Temple of Athena Pronaia at Delphi

Uncovering Delphi

Then, in the 1890s, archaeologists decided to **excavate** ancient Delphi. To do so, they had to move an entire village of people who were living on top of the ancient site. They built new homes for the villagers, demolished the old village and started to dig deep into the earth. The archaeologists found buildings and thousands of objects that tell us about life in ancient Greece.

An ancient Greek helmet found at Delphi

Words From History

The ancient Greeks not only wrote on papyrus (ancient paper) but they also carved long texts called inscriptions onto stone. They wanted these texts to last a long time, and they have – over 2500 years!

An inscription found at Delphi

Who Were the Ancient Greeks?

Ancient Greece was never an empire, like the **Roman Empire**, or a single country, like the modern United Kingdom. Instead, it was a community made up of more than 1000 different **city states** and a number of different tribal groups. A city state was known as a *polis*.

The ancient Greeks spread out around the Mediterranean Sea.

Front

A silver coin from the city state of Athens. Each city state produced its own money.

Back

The ancient Greeks spent a lot of time fighting. They fought among themselves – city state against city state. They also fought their major enemy the Persian Empire and in later times, the Romans.

This book looks at the period of ancient Greek history that began in the 9th century BC (800s BC) until the 2nd century BC when Greece became part of the Roman Empire.

Life in Ancient Greece

Life in Ancient Greece was very hard. About 25 percent of babies died in their first year, and many children never reached adulthood.

In some parts of Greece, such as Sparta, ancient texts tell us that babies were tested to see if they were strong and healthy. A baby was bathed in wine and then examined. If it was not strong, it was thrown off the top of a mountain to its death!

A small child's potty and highchair

A *hydria* (water jar) showing women collecting water from a fountain

Dirt and Disease

In cities, some people went to the toilet in the street, while others used a special pot that was then emptied onto the street. Water was collected from fountains, but also from rivers that could be polluted with sewage. Poverty, dirty water and bad **sanitation** caused stomach illnesses, tuberculosis, malaria and outbreaks of plague.

Praying for Help

Because the ancient Greeks were often at war, many people lived with terrible battle injuries. One medical record tells of how an arrow wound seeped 40 bowls of pus! The ancient Greeks had some understanding of medicine and surgery. Often, however, the best a sick or injured person could do was pray to their gods to be healed.

A model of an injured body part, called a votive, was offered to the gods when praying for a cure.

Figs

Wheat

Honey

Food in Ancient Greece

Most ordinary people ate a simple diet of cereals, vegetables, fruit and lots of olive oil. Fish was sometimes eaten, but could be very expensive. Meat was a luxury that was mostly eaten at big religious festivals.

Marrows

Plums

Lentils

Asparagus

Olives

Slaves

Life was particularly hard for slaves. In the city state of Athens, there were more than 100,000 slaves. They worked on farms, as teachers and in the Athenians' homes. They also worked for the city in silver mines and **quarries**. Bought in slave markets or captured in war, slaves were owned by their masters and had very little say in what they did or how they lived.

If you survived childhood and escaped illness and injury you might live to be 70 years old. A small number of ancient Greeks even made it to 100 years of age.

Lessons for Life

The kind of education you received in ancient Greece depended a lot on where you lived.

Time to Learn

In Athens, boys might be educated at home by a tutor. They studied music, **literature** and mathematics. They went to a gymnasium to exercise, wrestle and learn how to fight as warriors.

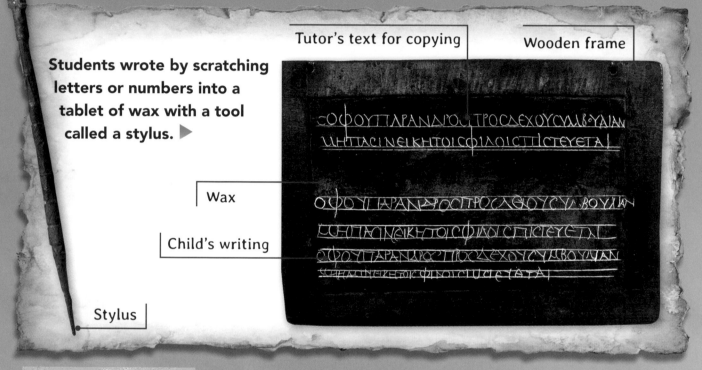

Students wrote by scratching letters or numbers into a tablet of wax with a tool called a stylus. ▶

Tutor's text for copying

Wooden frame

Wax

Child's writing

Stylus

Ready for War

In Sparta, boys were taken away from their families when they were seven. They lived in camps where they trained to be warriors — until the age of 30! To toughen them up, the boys had to forage for their own food and spend time living outside in the cold, with little clothing.

Men at Work in Ancient Greece

In Sparta male **citizens** were banned by law from having any profession except that of a soldier. The entire city state was one professional army. In Athens, however, the men did many different jobs. They worked as farmers, fishermen, stone masons, **architects**, playwrights and **merchants**. Athenian men only became soldiers when Athens was at war.

A Brave Thief

Spartan boys were encouraged to steal. During a war they might have to steal food to survive. Stealing also taught them to be daring. If a boy was caught, he was punished for being a failure. One famous story tells of a boy who stole a fox. When one of his adult trainers confronted him, the boy hid the fox beneath his clothes. The boy refused to reveal the fox even when it started to bite him. Eventually the boy died from his wounds, but he never admitted his crime!

Education for Girls

An Athenian girl's education took place at home and was overseen by her mother. She learned how to run the household and do tasks such as cooking and sewing.

Spartan girls were taught maths and literature. This was because Spartan women often helped run their city state when the men were away fighting. Spartan girls also took part in athletic competitions.

A 2500-year-old bronze statue of a Spartan girl athlete

Trainer

A mother visits the camp to watch her son training

Spartan boys at a training camp

Death in Ancient Greece

When ancient Greeks died, those they left behind followed a special funeral process.

The Lying Out

First, the body of the dead person was washed and laid out in the family home. Family members came to see the deceased and pay their respects. This was called the *prothesis*, which means "the lying out".

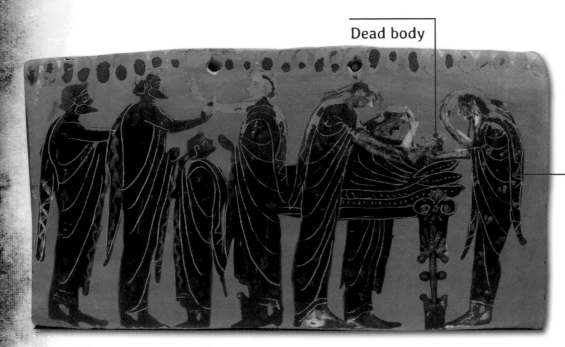

Dead body

The female mourners tear at their hair.

The Carrying Out

Then, after several days, family and friends carried the body through the streets to the burial ground. This funeral procession was called the *ekphora*, which means "the carrying out".

This ancient Greek *krater* (a jug used for mixing water with wine) shows an *ekphora* taking place. ▶

Mourners

Procession

The Funeral

At the city graveyard, the body was laid in a grave with important mementoes from the person's life, such as jewellery, clothing, weapons and drinking cups. The mourners then poured wine into the ground for the dead person. Once the grave was filled in, they often sat at the graveside and ate a simple meal.

The City's Dead

In ancient Athens, the city's graveyard, called the *kerameikos*, surrounded some of the main entrances to the city. Today, we usually only go into a cemetery if we are visiting a grave. In ancient Athens, however, everyone arriving or leaving had to walk through the city's dead!

Modern-day Athens

The remains of the kerameikos

Tombstones Tell a Story

In the ancient cemetery in Athens there are many enormous and ornate tombstones. Sometimes they display not only the name of the person and a dedication from their family, but a beautiful image of the deceased doing something from their lifetime.

In Sparta, people did not have ornate tombstones. A man got his name on his grave only if he died in a war. A woman was remembered only if she died in childbirth. Everyone else was buried in an unmarked grave.

The tombstone of a shoemaker named Xanthippos

Gods and Goddesses

Aphrodite
Goddess of love

Apollo
God of light and the Sun

Hera
Queen of the gods

The Ancient Greeks did not believe in just one god. They believed in the presence of many gods in their lives.

The Olympians

The most powerful of this vast family of gods were the 12 gods who lived on Mount Olympus. The Olympian gods were led by Zeus, king of the gods, and his wife Hera.

Pleasing the Gods

The ancient Greeks believed that their gods could help them and harm them. The gods could even kill a person they didn't like or stop that person's plans coming to pass. This meant the ancient Greeks spent lots of time trying to please their gods.

Zeus
King of the gods

A Barbecue for the Gods

One way that the ancient Greeks pleased their gods was by **sacrificing** animals such as oxen, cows, sheep and goats. Then they burned the bones and fatty parts of the animals on an **altar**. It was said that the gods loved the smoke that came from the burning of animal fat and bones. The rest of the meat (all the good bits) was cooked for the people to eat. This meant an ancient Greek religious festival often turned into a giant barbecue!

Offering Dedications

The Ancient Greeks tried to please their gods by offering them dedications. A dedication could be small and personal, like a favourite cup placed in a god's sanctuary. It could also be large and showy. Some people built expensive buildings called treasuries as an offering to the gods.

Each of the Olympian gods was responsible for one or more areas of ancient Greek life.

Poseidon
God of the seas

Advice From the Gods

The ancient Greeks also asked questions of their gods. They could do this in a variety of ways.

Some priests could pass on the thoughts of the gods by listening to the rustling of tree leaves or by rolling a dice. Some could read signs hidden in the entrails of animals. And sometimes the gods were thought to speak directly to people through a priest or priestess called an oracle.

The gods' answers helped people decide what to do in their lives. It also let them know if the gods were looking down on them with favour.

It was believed that an oracle (priestess) could speak the words of the gods.

Ancient Architecture

Ancient Greek architects and builders designed and built many incredible structures.

This cutaway diagram shows the Temple of Zeus at Olympia

Building for the Gods

The most important structure at a religious sanctuary was the altar. This was where people sacrificed animals and burnt offerings to the gods.

Oxen for sacrifice

Altar

Next in importance was the temple, which was a large, expensive building made in marble or limestone with columns all around the outside. The temple housed the statue of the god or goddess to whom the sanctuary was dedicated.

The Parthenon

At the centre of modern-day Athens stands the Parthenon, a temple that was built 2500 years ago. Every column bends inwards just a tiny amount. If the columns continued upwards into the sky, they would all meet 2.4 kilometres up in the air. It's incredible to think that ancient Greek architects and builders were able to achieve this with only calculations and tools – no computers or machinery!

The Parthenon is part of the Acropolis, a fortified group of religious buildings on a hillside overlooking Athens.

The statue of Zeus was 13 metres tall.

The ancient Greeks built many theatres. In these theatres, plays were performed to honour the god of theatre and wine, Dionysus. In Athens during the main religious festival of Dionysus, all public business in the city shut down. Everyone was expected to go to the theatre to watch plays in honour of the god.

▲ This theatre at Delphi was built into the hillside and could seat 5000 people.

The walls were up to 10 m high.

Athens

Walls for Defence

Ancient Greek cities were often surrounded by a large, defensive wall. The people of Athens built walls not just around the city, but also as a huge walled corridor between the city and its seaport, known as the Piraeus. These walls protected Athens against attack and ensured it could always bring in goods by sea for its citizens.

The walled corridor was about 6 km long.

15

The Olympic Games

The first-ever Olympic games were held in 776 BC.

Games for a King

The games were held in honour of Zeus and took place in and around the sanctuary of Zeus at a place called Olympia. Unlike the modern Olympics, the games were a form of religious worship. During the games 100 oxen would be sacrificed in a single go in honour of the king of the gods.

The Games

The events at the ancient Greek Olympics included running races, chariot racing, boxing and wrestling. Athletes competed on behalf of their home cities and the only prize was for first place.

In the running event called the *stadion*, competitors sprinted for 180 metres – barefoot and naked.

The *pankration* (which means "all power event") was a kind of wrestling match. The only rules were no gouging of the eyes or killing your opponent.

Tough on Spectators

Thousands of spectators gathered to watch the games. Don't imagine it was always a pleasant experience, though. In the heat of a Greek summer there would be around 40,000 people camped in tents plus the animals they brought along to eat. There were no toilets, only one river nearby for drinking water and washing, and the ground was soaked with blood from the slaughter of sacrificial animals. It was hot, smelly and noisy. In fact, one ancient writer suggested that if you wanted to punish a slave, you sent him to the Olympics!

In the *hoplitodromos* race, naked athletes ran wearing a helmet and carrying a shield.

Chariot racing

If you were a victorious athlete at the Olympic games, you could pay a poet to write a special poem about your own achievements!

Ancient Versus Modern

The ancient Olympic games were very different from today's Olympics.

• The games were always held in the same place at Olympia in Greece.

• Only Greeks could compete, unlike in today's games, which welcome athletes from across the world.

• Women were banned from competing and they weren't even allowed to watch the events.

Olive wreath

• The only prize was for first place – no silver or bronze medals. And instead of a gold medal the winners won a wreath made from an olive branch cut from the sacred olive tree of Zeus.

• Oh..........and most people competed naked!

Despite these differences, what the Greeks started 2700 years ago still continues today.

Politics and Democracy

The idea of democracy, which means "the power of the demos (or people)" began in ancient Greece.

Who Was in Charge?

In ancient Greece, there were more than 1000 city states and some tribal communities. Each one controlled its own territory. Some communities were ruled by monarchies, others by tyrants — rulers who had taken power for themselves.

Many were ruled by oligarchies, which means "rule of the few". In these communities power was in the hands of a small group of normally older citizens. A few city states were run as democracies. The most famous of these was Athens.

Hello! I'm Democracy

Democracy came into existence in Athens some time after 508 BC. But it would take until the 460s BC (about 40 years) before people called their system of government "democracy". The idea and word were so popular that people even gave "Democracy" to their children as a first name!

One Man, One Vote

Democracy in Athens was based on the simple idea that every male citizen should have an equal say in the running of their city state. Each man would also be equal in the eyes of the law. The men met on the Pnyx, a hill above Athens. An official called a herald was in charge and invited people to speak. Any man could give his opinion about an issue and then a vote was taken with a show of hands.

There was space on the Pnyx for about 6000 people.

Ancient Issues

Voters would debate major issues such as whether to go to war. They also made decisions about building new ships or temples. They might even vote on whether to exile, or banish, a citizen who was causing trouble in the democracy.

The person speaking stood on the speakers' platform.

Democracy in Action

Today, the ancient democracy at Athens might seem quite undemocratic to us. It did not give the vote to women or to foreigners who lived in Athens. And it was a political system that allowed slavery.

But it's important to remember that the ancient Athenians would not think our modern systems of democracy were very democratic either. They believed every male citizen should meet, discuss, debate and vote on every issue. This was a direct democracy.

In the UK, voters elect representatives, called Members of Parliament (MPs), to make decisions for them in the Houses of Parliament. This is an indirect or representative democracy.

The word "politics" comes from the ancient Greek *ta politika*, which means "the affairs of the city".

The herald roughly counted the number of hands, or made a good guess.

19

Ancient Greek Art

The ancient Greeks surrounded themselves with statues, carvings, wall paintings and decorated pots.

Honouring the Gods

Today we call these objects art. However, the ancient Greeks did not think of these creations as decorative objects to be hung on a wall or viewed in a museum. Most art in ancient Greece was created for an important purpose, such as honouring a god.

This is a life-size, modern-day reconstruction of the statue of Athena.

The statue was 11.5 metres tall.

A giant statue of Athena once stood inside the Parthenon. Athena was the goddess of wisdom and war. A sculptor named Phidias created the statue from ivory, silver and gold.

Saying Thank You

A statue of a man (usually naked) or a woman (always clothed) would be placed in a god's sanctuary in thanks for a victory in battle or success in business. Statues might even be erected in advance of a war to try to win the gods' support.

A wealthy citizen or the leaders of a city would pay a sculptor to carve a statue or a decorative **frieze**.

Olympic Heroes

Following victories at the Olympic games, cities often erected statues of their winning athletes. The statues usually showed the athlete naked and with incredible muscles.

Just as airbrushing and Photoshop are used to change the appearance of models today, ancient Greek sculptors made the bodies of sport stars look perfect!

A carving from a frieze around the Parthenon

Today we think of marble sculptures and carvings as being white, but they were originally painted bright colours. The ancient paint has flaked away, leaving just the marble underneath.

Statues were sculpted from marble, bronze or ivory.

An Olympic discus thrower

Everyday Art

Sometimes, a pair of eyes was painted on the side of a drinking cup.

The ancient Greeks made thousands and thousands of drinking cups, jugs and other containers. They were painted with battle scenes and images of athletic competitions and **myths**. The cups and jugs were made for use in the *symposium*. This was a wine-drinking and talking party that regularly took place in Greek homes.

This eye cup shows the story of Theseus, who killed the Minotaur, a half-man half-bull monster.

21

Poems, Plays and Philosophy

The ancient Greeks were writers of **epic poems** and plays. They also wrote about science, history and **philosophy**.

A statue of the philosopher Socrates

Great Storytellers

In ancient Greece, plays and poems nearly always focused on one of the Greek myths. The myths were a huge collection of stories about gods, heroes and monstrous creatures. The stories also featured human kings, queens, sorcerers and soothsayers, people who could see into the future.

Understanding the World

Some ancient Greeks chose to study and write about philosophy. Philosophers dedicated their lives to seeking greater wisdom and trying to understand humankind and the world around them.

Ancient Greek philosophers often asked difficult questions, such as: *What does it mean to live a good life?* Sometimes, they were admired. But at other times people thought they made life very difficult because they were always asking why!

The word philosophy comes from *philos*, meaning "love of something", and *sophia*, meaning "wisdom".

The Power of Oratory

Some ancient Greeks were skilled at **oratory**. They could make powerful speeches that convinced people to agree with their point of view. Some great orators wrote down their political or legal speeches so they would not be forgotten.

Socrates

One of the most famous ancient Greek philosophers was an Athenian called Socrates. He often annoyed people by showing them how their arguments did not make sense.

In fact, Socrates upset his fellow citizens so much that some of them brought a legal case against him. He was found guilty of a number of charges and was sentenced to death by poisoning!

We still enjoy ancient Greek myths today. In this scene from the movie *Troy* Greek soldiers gain access to Troy by hiding inside a giant wooden horse that the Trojans believe is a gift. ▼

The Iliad and The Odyssey

Two of the greatest epic poems are the *Iliad* and the *Odyssey*. These stories centre on the mythical Trojan War between the Greeks and the city of Troy. The poems are credited to the poet Homer.

The *Iliad* is set during the 10-year siege of Troy by the Greeks. It tells the story of the great warrior hero Achilles.

The *Odyssey* focuses on the efforts of the Greek hero Odysseus to return home after 10 years at Troy. During the journey, Odysseus blinds the one-eyed giant Polyphemus, who is the son of Poseidon, god of the sea.

Odysseus gets Polyphemus drunk so he can blind him.

It takes Odysseus 10 years to get home because Poseidon wants to punish him and prevent his return. This story shows what can happen when the gods are against you!

The Greco-Persian Wars

The ancient Greeks had always fought among themselves. But in the 5th century BC, the city states joined forces to fight the mighty Persian Empire.

The Battle of Marathon

In 490 BC, the king of the Persian Empire, King Darius, and about 30,000 soldiers landed in the bay of Marathon, near Athens. With the odds hugely stacked against them, about 10,000 Athenian **hoplites** faced Darius's army. In a daring attack, the Athenian soldiers charged and surrounded the invaders. They killed 6400 Persians and forced Darius's army to retreat and sail home.

The First Marathon

An Athenian soldier ran all the way from Marathon to Athens (a distance of about 42 kilometres) to announce the Athenian victory. More than 2000 years later, this momentous run would be the inspiration for a modern athletic event – the marathon!

The Battle of Thermopylae

In 480 BC, Darius's son, King Xerxes, brought a massive force by land and sea to Greece. At first the Persian advance was held back by the Greek army at a narrow mountain pass called Thermopylae. At the forefront of the fighting were King Leonidas of Sparta and 300 Spartan warriors.

Spartan warriors

Persian soldiers

The Spartans fought to the death, holding the Persians at bay for as long as possible. After killing the Spartans, the Persian forces marched on through Greece and even burnt Athens to the ground.

A Greek *hoplite* soldier

The Battle of Salamis

Later in 480 BC, the Greeks won a great sea battle in a narrow waterway, called the straits of Salamis. About 300 Greek warships trapped the Persian fleet of around 600 ships. The Greeks sank hundreds of their enemy's ships by ramming them.

Finally, a year later, at the battle of Plataea, the Greek army defeated the Persians once again, forcing them to retreat back to Persia.

In sea battles, the metal ram of a Greek *triremes* warship was used to smash holes in the sides of enemy ships.

The ship was rowed by 170 men.

Victorious!

Their victories in war had a deep impact on the ancient Greeks. Their triumphs gave them a sense of confidence and pride in their ability to work together to defend themselves. But it did not last for long. Soon the Greek city states were fighting with one another once again.

A Democratic Decision

When the Persians invaded Greece in 480 BC, the Athenians debated what to do. They decided with a democratic vote to evacuate Athens. Old men, women and children were taken to safety on the islands of Troezen and Salamis.

Ancient Greek Explorers

The ancient Greeks loved to explore. They sailed throughout the Mediterranean trading and searching for new places to settle.

New Settlements

From the 8th century BC onwards the Greeks created cities in southern Italy, Sicily, Spain and France. The modern city of Marseille in France began its history as the ancient Greek settlement of Massalia. The ancient Greeks also settled on the north coast of Africa in Egypt and modern-day Libya.

A replica of an ancient Greek merchant's ship

Wine and olive oil were transported in jars called *amphorae*.

Merchants and Trade

Ancient Greek merchants sailed and traded throughout the Mediterranean. They sold beautiful pottery, bronze objects, olives, wine, olive oil, figs, meat, cheese, honey, perfume and even marble. Traders returned from their travels with goods that could be sold in the Greek *agoras*, or markets. These goods included gold, silver, iron, copper, textiles, cereals, spices – and even slaves.

Proud Greeks

All the Greek settlements traded with each other and the city states back home in Greece. The settlers were proud of their Greek heritage and sent athletes to compete at the Olympic games. They also took part in Greek wars, sending soldiers to fight enemies, such as the Persians, and when the Greek city states were fighting against one another.

Alexander the Great Conqueror and Explorer

Alexander the Great goes into battle in a scene from the movie *Alexander*

In the 4th century BC, Alexander the Great, the king of Macedon (a Greek kingdom) led an army into the east. He conquered the Persian Empire and marched on through Asia to the banks of the River Indus in India and modern-day Pakistan.

As a result of Alexander's conquests, Greek settlements grew up as far east as Afghanistan, and Greek **culture** was spread far and wide throughout the ancient world. The modern-day city of Kandahar, in Afghanistan, was originally a settlement created by Alexander the Great. Some ancient Greeks even made their homes in northern India.

The Explorer Pytheas

Around 330 BC, a Greek explorer named Pytheas embarked on a daring journey. He set off from the Greek port of Massalia, sailed out of the Mediterranean into the Atlantic Ocean and headed up towards Britain. Historians believe Pytheas was the first ancient Greek to visit and sail around Britain. He landed in Cornwall to explore and see its tin mines. He even sailed up into the Arctic Circle and saw the ocean waters freeze into ice.

Ancient Greece in Our World

It's hard to believe that a civilisation which lived so long ago could still impact our lives today. But the ancient Greeks do.

The Romans and Ancient Greece

In some ways this is because the ancient Greeks had a huge impact on the Romans. In the 2nd Century BC the Romans conquered Greece and it became part of the Roman Empire. The Romans thought of themselves as superior to the Greeks in military matters. But they always felt that the Greeks were superior to them in terms of culture.

The British Museum in London looks like an ancient Greek temple, but it was built in the 1800s.

Ancient Greece Comes to Britain

The Romans praised Greek art, architecture, literature and philosophy. They **preserved** Greek texts, art and buildings which we can still see today. And when the Romans invaded Britain, they brought ideas from ancient Greece with them.

The Father of History

The ancient Greek writer Herodotus wrote an account of the Greco-Persian wars called *The Histories*. Herodotus collected stories and eyewitness reports of the battles. Then he used this information to try to understand the events before writing about them. No one had ever written history in this way before and Herodotus became known as "the father of history".

The Greek
hero Perseus

The head of
the Medusa

This bronze statue was
made at a time called the
Renaissance, in the 1500s.
Renaissance sculptors
copied the ancient Greek
way of creating detailed,
realistic statues.

Not Ancient History

The ancient Greeks gave
the world democracy,
great art, theatre, the Olympic Games
and important ideas in maths, science
and philosophy. Today we still admire the
many skills of the ancient Greeks and their
civilisation still influences our modern world.

Many countries around the
world have a democratic
system of government and
democracy is considered one
of the great achievements in
our whole human story.

Words For All Time

We are still able to read the ancient
Greeks' extraordinary poems, plays
and other texts today. The Greeks
wrote with great power about
emotions and ideas such as love, hate,
justice, freedom and revenge. And the
incredible things they had to say are
still important to people today.

Glossary

altar
A large table or flat-topped, table-like block of stone used in a religious ceremony for making sacrifices or offerings to a god.

archaeologist
A scientist who studies the past by examining the physical remains left behind, for example, buildings, skeletons and artefacts such as coins and weapons.

architect
A person who designs and manages the construction of buildings and other structures.

citizen
In ancient Greece, a free male (not a slave) aged over 18. Only citizens were allowed to vote.

city state
A city and its surrounding villages and land in ancient Greece. The ancient Greek word for "city state" was *polis*.

culture
The beliefs and way of life of a group of people. For example, traditions, celebrations, art and food are all part of a group's culture.

democracy
A system of government that allows people to vote for their representatives or leaders and have a say in the running of their country.

epic poem
A very long dramatic story that's written as a poem in verses and features lots of different characters and places.

excavate
To dig out or remove something from soil or rock.

frieze
A broad band of sculpted or painted decorations on a building.

hoplite
An ancient Greek foot soldier from one of the city states. A *hoplite* carried a spear and shield.

literature
Written works such as poems, plays and books.

merchant
A person (usually from history) who buys and sells goods. Merchants often travelled from place to place to do business.

myth
A traditional story that includes popular beliefs or explains a particular event or natural phenomena.

oratory
The activity of giving skilful speeches in public that can win arguments.

philosophy
A way of thinking (and asking questions) about the world, the universe and humankind.

preserve
Protect something, such as a building, and stop it from being damaged or destroyed.

quarry
A large deep hole from which rock, such as marble, is dug out.

Roman Empire
The parts of the world that were conquered and ruled over by the Romans. The empire included Italy and parts of Europe, North Africa and the Middle East.

sacrifice
To kill an animal or person as part of a ritual or as an offering to a god.

sanctuary
A place, building or group of buildings where people worshipped one or more gods.

sanitation
Anything to do with having clean drinking water and the hygienic removal of sewage.

texts
Books or other written works, such as speeches, plays or historical records.

Index